"As I move i
husband I ar
never seems
source of comfort and company for me.

...I never knew someone could write with so much understanding and compassion. Much of what she expressed mirrored so much of what I was dealing with... I am truly blessed."

- *Patricia Paulson, lost her soul-mate two years ago to cancer*

"Our Healing Hearts Grief Support Group journeyed with you on a most turbulent voyage. Your book taught us that we were not alone; to take time to breathe, let the process unfold, and that healing is a choice. We also learned that it takes courage to step into our pain, but if we trust the process we will eventually arrive in calm waters.

That is where healing takes place. Thank you for gifting us with your poetic and insightful words."

- *Richard W. Amend, M.Ed., Director of Senior Adult Ministry and Myrna Hicks (co-facilitator) of Christ the King Catholic Church, Oklahoma City, OK*

"My daughter, Erin, was born premature. Despite everyone's best efforts, she passed on after 7 hours of Life. For those 7 hours she lay in my wife's arms and mine. Not many people can say they lived a life completely surrounded by Love. She did. Eighteen months later we were blessed with a baby boy. I know Erin watches closely over him and us. Bev's heartwarming books and monthly messages have eased the pain of my loss. Thank you Bev, from the bottom of my heart."

- *Scott Paton. A father who lost a baby daughter. An Internet Marketing Mentor.*

"Bev has reached deep inside herself to reveal the true depth and power of her own grief. In sharing her heartfelt writings with others, she's given name to the unnamable sorrows and the uncontrollable feelings that are a part of grieving. Her poetic voice will resonate with all who have lost a loved one."
- *Kim Stacey, anthropologist/writer.*

"Bev's book, *"Wide My Ocean, Deep My Grief"* helps us to see life and grief through many lenses: with our eye, with our mind, with our intuition, but most importantly how to see with our hearts. In the aftermath of any loss, Bev helps us to begin to re-examine and redefine ourselves, our values and our possibilities in very ordinary, human ways until a new life begins to emerge for us. Bev's personal story of grief, her poetry and her reflections are realistic and universal. She inspires through her own appreciation of the grief journey and of the joy of living."
- *Adele Roy, CPE Specialist with Canadian Association for Pastoral Practice and Education. She has ministered to many grieving people through her extensive hospital ministry in Pastoral Care.*

Supplementary Grieving Resources available at http://www.copewithgrieving.com
"Please visit my grieving support website to request your free subscription to my monthly e-mail connection letter. You may also view (or even contribute to) the selections of Grieving Stories Shared. Finally, you can read the latest Weekly Inspirational or even view past weeks Inspirationals (link near the top of website). I look forward to connecting with you and supporting you in this way."
- *Bev Swanson, author of "Wide My Ocean, Deep My Grief"*

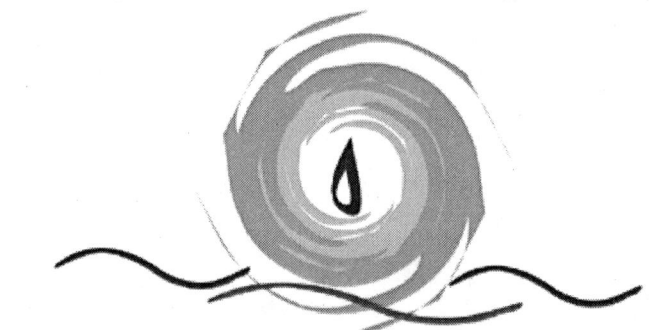

Wide my Ocean, Deep my Grief

a gentle guide thru the uncharted waters of the grieving process

Wide My Ocean, Deep My Grief

"A gentle, personal guide thru the uncharted waters of the grieving process."

By Bev Swanson

Layout Design by Rosa Bohnet

I dedicate this book to our daughter,

Jayde Mikayla,

our precious gem who lived life large and gifted us immensely.

Thank you little one.

© Copyright 2005 Bev Swanson
www.copewithgrieving.com

All rights reserved. No part of this publication may be reproduced, stored in a retrieval system, or transmitted, in any form or by any means, electronic, mechanical, photocopying, recording, or otherwise, without the written prior permission of the author.

Note for Librarians: A cataloguing record for this book is available from Library and Archives Canada at www.collectionscanada.ca/amicus/index-e.html
ISBN 1-4120-6966-1

Printed in Victoria, BC, Canada. Printed on paper with minimum 30% recycled fibre. Trafford's print shop runs on "green energy" from solar, wind and other environmentally-friendly power sources.

TRAFFORD
PUBLISHING

Offices in Canada, USA, Ireland and UK

This book was published *on-demand* in cooperation with Trafford Publishing. On-demand publishing is a unique process and service of making a book available for retail sale to the public taking advantage of on-demand manufacturing and Internet marketing. On-demand publishing includes promotions, retail sales, manufacturing, order fulfilment, accounting and collecting royalties on behalf of the author.

Book sales for North America and international:
Trafford Publishing, 6E–2333 Government St.,
Victoria, BC v8t 4p4 CANADA
phone 250 383 6864 (toll-free 1 888 232 4444)
fax 250 383 6804; email to orders@trafford.com

Book sales in Europe:
Trafford Publishing (uk) Limited, 9 Park End Street, 2nd Floor
Oxford, UK ox1 1hh UNITED KINGDOM
phone 44 (0)1865 722 113 (local rate 0845 230 9601)
facsimile 44 (0)1865 722 868; info.uk@trafford.com

Order online at:
trafford.com/05-1877

10 9 8 7 6 5 4 3

Table of Contents

The Birthing of a Book

Foreword i

Chapter One: Bon Voyage
"The Final Goodbye" 1

Chapter Two: Shipwrecked
"The Tearing, Wrenching Few Moments
and Days Just After..." 21

Chapter Three: Riding the Waves
"An Emotional Roller Coaster" 45

Chapter Four: Getting our Bearings
"Settling into our Grieving" 61

Chapter Five: Harbour Days
"Bittersweet and Special Days" 77

Chapter Six: Shipmates
"Our Companions on the Journey" 91

Chapter Seven: Finding Dry Land
"Living with Death" 105

In Closing - Tributes 127

In Closing - For Your Journey 133

In Closing - Final Poem 139

Wide my Ocean, Deep my Grief

THE BIRTHING OF A BOOK

The writing of this book has come naturally but not always with ease as it brings up the pain of our loss once again. This book has been in process for a couple of years now. It is as though the feelings and experiences have been waiting deep within me, almost as if I were pregnant. They have grown, formed and found root; yet the words have waited, until now.

It is now time to give birth to this book. It is time to release my thoughts, ideas and experiences into the world. They are released to you who hurt so deeply; in the hopes that my sharing will help. This guide to a path of healing, comfort, hope, and new life is available to any who are open to it.

Interestingly, the other day I opened my journal to an entry I made over a year ago. I was writing of the importance of opening to what I was to do in life and making room for what was next for me. I said in the very next entry and I quote:

"I still want to write a book and speak our story to help others - but first I will help myself to be open to God for my own healing. The rest will come."

About a year ago, I began to sense that enough healing had come to my soul. I am now ready to share with you our story of deep grief and deep healing. May these pages of poetry, story, prose and reflection bless you in your journey, bringing some peace into the "Ocean of your Grief".

Foreword

Oh grieving one
I cry with you

My soul knows how deep your pain.
And so I write...and share my soul...

...that you may stand again
...that you may be understood - not so alone
...that you may know how precious you are

precious enough to breathe and heal
from the deep, deep ocean of your grief

and enter once again
into the dance of living.

For Your Company and Hope

I am not a stranger to grieving and although my experience is mine and yours is yours, I share with you my grieving place so that you may find some company and in that company some hope.

Since you are reading this, you have likely found yourself in a painful grieving space or are travelling with one who is grieving. It is my desire that by sharing some of our story, coupled with the knowledge I have acquired from journeying with others, you may find hope, comfort, and even some joy in the midst of your pain and loss.

Perhaps you may feel less alone and feel a bit more understood in your process. Perhaps you will find some sliver of hope that you will one day find dry land after being tossed into so deep and tumultuous ocean.

Trip Through Deep Ocean Waters
It has been my experience that the journey through death and loss is not unlike sailing the high seas and one day finding yourself tossed into cold angry waters abruptly, almost with no warning.

Along with many others, I felt as though I was being continuously washed over by huge waves of uncontrolled emotion. Suddenly, the sun would come out as if to mock me, followed just seconds later by another overwhelming wave of devastation.

After this I would find myself in a lifeboat with a hole in the bottom. I always find it so amazing that eventually through this turmoil, healing comes, lives mend and dry land appears again.

Foreword

Journey through Seven Grieving Spaces

Somehow, it seems fitting for me to write this book using the analogy of a trip through the deep ocean waters. These waters are unpredictable, frightening, cold, and lonely at times, along with a vast collection of other feelings.

It can be a pretty lonely and terrifying situation to be in the ocean, so vast and deep, with no sign of shore. So is the journey through the grieving places. I felt as though the ocean of my grief was so deep I would never get to the bottom of it.

In this book, the grieving process has been broken into 7 important places we found ourselves occupying while struggling with the loss of our daughter (or seven stages if you will).

Each chapter begins with a poem, and a piece of our story, which is followed by some personal and professional reflections. You will notice in our story that grieving is never a linear process but it changes and transforms as it cycles over time.

Book of the "Heart"

This is a book of the "heart". You will find a lot of information "about" grieving tucked amidst our story and my reflections. Primarily, I set out to keep you company in your pain and encourage your healing on a heart and soul level. It will be helpful to have a guide for your grieving journey.

If you are looking for right answers or quick fixes you will not find them here. There are no right answers for so difficult a journey. There are only good choices, quiet understandings and some helpful ways to take the next step or breathe the next breath.

One very important point to remember is that everyone is unique in their process. Indeed there are some things about our story that will seem familiar to you and will likely strike some painful chords for you. However, you will have a unique story and a unique process that will bring you healing.

Your Unique and Sacred Journey
Your process is an important and sacred journey. Honour it as unique and precious, just as you are unique and precious. Give yourself all the space you need, as you do what you need to do, to heal.

Your healing is your process. So as you listen to our process, honour your own and let it be what it is. If somehow the sharing of our story can aid in that healing and be present to your process we are honoured.

You may find while reading this that you need to read it in small pieces or put it down for a time to pick it up again. I encourage you to listen to what you need and what your soul can handle. Sometimes I found I had to read things slowly or even more than once, in order for me to receive the help I so longed for.

Honour your Process
Certainly I wish that you would not find yourself victimized by death like so many do. Dare to imagine that you will be able to move through the pain of your loss into a place where death has made you richer. Hopefully, you can see you have some choices even in such a painful and in some ways, unforgiving process. Above all, know that you are not alone in these choices.

As I share with you a bit of my healing process it is important to name that this has been a very spiritual journey for me. One of trusting that the healer of my broken heart and soul would indeed bring me to healing. I did not always recognize God's presence. At times I even felt like I had been abandoned in the midst of the most incredibly painful part of my life.

Intense Healing Love
Yet I was being held in the deep arms of God; the healer of my pain. This love came often in ways

that I did not expect at all. I experienced that God weeps with us and holds us in many various ways. I sensed God reaching out to me in the midst of the ocean of my grief, offering presence and healing.

May your process lead you back to dry land where your feet can be planted safely on the ground. It is my prayer that you will remain open to the healing that is yours, if you want it. May you enter fully into the dance of life in the midst of death.

Dance with Life in the Midst of Death
During our time together may you find understanding, love, and peace in the midst of the storm. May you find hope as you venture out into this vast ocean of grief to your place of healing.

God, you gifted us with our little Jayde. When she could not stay here with us; you allowed her to teach us, open us and remind us what life is all about. You used her life and leaving, to remind us of your great love. We are continually reminded to enter more fully into the dance of life, even in our void.

To Our Precious Jayde Mikayla
Jayde Mikayla... precious gem... we waited for you with such joyful anticipation. We had no idea just what an incredible gift you would be for us. Your

gift came in disguise and at first we couldn't see the gift for the pain.

Your presence and your painful leaving taught us to live life more fully in the moment. From you we learned to trust deeply, to feel openly, to love when love is risky and to dance, even when our feet were dragging. You lived so closely to your maker and you brought us into that closeness even more deeply.

We will always miss you, our precious Jayde. Impatiently, we wait for the day when we will be reunited. We are deeply grateful for your time with us, although it was so very brief.

We have grown to be grateful for the void you left us in. This void makes us eternally open to the "Lover of our Souls".

It allows us to journey more fully with others in their pain.

Best of all, we had the chance to love you and be loved by you.

Jayde... We will always miss you at our table, on our holidays, on our celebrations, and every day. My soul longs for you... to hold you. Yet I will always, always hold you in my heart.

Thank you my baby, my wise, wise little baby girl. May you find dancing shoes in heaven until we are able to dance with you there.

Chapter 1

Bon Voyage

"The Final Goodbye"

I love you so...

and I fear that you will leave me
...soon...too soon...
and I won't be ready

I will say good-bye but
my good-bye will never be enough
for me...

Because I do not want you to go
at all...
it is not time yet...

I must savour our moments because
we have today...

And today is enough...
and yet not near enough...

I love you so...
please know this...
even if
my good-bye is less than perfect.

SHARING OUR STORY

As a counsellor, I have walked with many through the valley of death. All of your experiences have taught me so much about grieving. Yet no experience so poignantly as the journey through our own precious little daughter's life and death, as well as the untimely death of dear friends.

Visited by Death
I never knew the incredible path we would find ourselves on when we decided to have children. In fact all of it has been coupled with grief. Our son, Brendyn, now 7, was born with Down Syndrome. Then we miscarried a baby and never got to actually see that child face to face. Both of these experiences came with a great deal of pain.

Our third child, Jayde Mikayla, also came to us with a mix of joy and sorrow. Our journey with Jayde has been our deepest experience of pain. I can feel in my soul the intense feelings she brings even in the mention of her name.

We waited for Jayde's coming with all the same joyful anticipation that many parents await the coming of new child. We love parenting and knew this would be no different.

Precious Child is Born

Jayde was born on a wintry January morning. There was a stillness in my soul the night before, almost like a calm before the storm. I sensed something was coming but brushed it away, chalking it up to nervousness. The c-section surgery went as planned but the rest of the day became a blur. They rushed our little one away.

In what seemed like just a short time later, Dale came back with the doctor. He was carrying our precious bundle with tears streaming down his face. She was expected to live only a few minutes. I burst into tears. I only remember saying, "I cannot do this again! Why do I have to do this again?!"

Not Expected to Live

The next few days became almost like living in a calm storm. Our little Jayde did not die right away. In fact she stayed with us for 22 precious, wonderful and difficult days.

We decided that our little girl deserved to be loved to the depths of her soul from the depths of our soul even if her leaving would tear us in two. So we spent a few days in the hospital. We bonded with her. We held her and cuddled her, shared her with friends, baptized her.

Her baptism was very sacred to us. Sitting quietly in a room with our friends, one of whom was a pastor. In that moment, it became clear this was the time to baptize her.

Simple Ceremony
It was a simple ceremony yet beautiful in its' simplicity. Our pastor friend used the distilled water from one of the numerous little sealed jars nearby. A nurse quickly found us a Bible from some other place. There in that simple little space...in the silent holy moment, she received the gift of baptism. A special time we got to share with her.

We wanted her to be blessed in her baptism. In this way she could know and experience the incredible feeling of being loved intensely by God. In this time God seemed to not only hold her, but also held all of us sitting in that holy moment.

With God's help we breathed life into her. Dale would sit at the little window near her bed and show her the snow and tell her about skiing and snow and winter. I held her in the hospital room while she and I slept.

Dancing with Death

There were times of celebration. Friends and family came by the hospital to celebrate her arrival and to support us. In addition, there were the ups and downs when she would seem to be dancing with death. She would stop breathing only to rally up the strength to keep on going. Such dreadful moments, as we waited to see if she would come back to us.

The kindness of my doctor, her doctor and all the nurses was so clear in their loving support. They took such tender care of her. After all, they all wished this was different. Yet I think she blessed them with her presence.

With Tender Gentle Care

The day came to take her home. Terrified and relieved, we bundled her up for that long drive home in the dead of winter's night. We had the care of a special nurse, who so tenderly and carefully wrapped her in the car seat, to keep her comfortable and safe.

We will never forget the attention she gave to this task. She showed us beyond measure just how valued and important this little life was. This meant the world to us that someone else gently cared for her with such value.

Chapter 1

The Journey Home

Setting out on this very cold night, we drove into the next leg of our journey. All the time we were afraid that something might happen on the road and we would have no one to help.

What mixed feelings we had; joy, sadness, fear, they went on and on. Instead of coming home to celebrate the expectancy of a full life together, we came home to the unknown. How long would this together time be? If it were a longer time, what would it look like?

In the back of our mind, we held the knowledge that death was a very possible outcome. Thankfully our pastor friend came as soon as we arrived home. Dale's Mom and Dad also met us, to help us cope with a new baby who was very sick.

Straddling Life and Death

She was so tiny, so peaceful and so perfect. We were happy, sad and so afraid. We were scared to hope that she would live and afraid to think she may leave us. It was difficult to straddle that line of life and death every waking minute.

At one point I said to a friend that I wasn't sure I could live like this much longer. He shared a really neat analogy with me. It went something like this. If life is in the bedroom and death in the hallway, just live in the bedroom because she is alive right now and that is where she is. When she goes she will lead the way into the hallway of death.

Somehow this helped me to just be with the truth of the moment and not think so much of the sorrow of the impending future.

Little Miracle
We had taken our little one home to love and to parent for as many days as we had. We hoped beyond all hopes that she would be our little miracle girl; and in way she was. She did so many of the things the doctors said she would never do.

She ate on her own, swallowed, cried, peed and pooped and she grew... Against all odds she grew! She had baths in our kitchen sink and gave us so much joy. She taught us to live in the moment, because we knew that the moment was all we could be sure to have with her.

We enjoyed our time sharing her. Friends came, as did relatives, siblings, and grandparents; all hoping our time with her would not be so brief. They showered her with gifts. We received them in joy but also in sorrow, as sometimes we were not sure she would live long enough to use them.

Daring to Hope

I remember going shopping with my mother; such a normal thing to do when a child is born. Over me hung a shadow. This shadow was one of the unknowns; pointing to the so very real possibility that she would not live long. Yet I dared to buy her things. I needed to hope she might survive. Besides she was still here.

Whenever I left the house I was afraid I would find her gone when I returned. It was as if I thought, that she would be safer if I stayed home.

Little Jayde lived with an oxygen tube, so we watched the colour in her face often. If she got a bit grey we would adjust the oxygen a bit, as we had been instructed. We celebrated the days when less oxygen seemed to be needed. I would check regularly in the night to see if her colour was ok. She slept on my chest during the night where my breathing would in turn remind her to breathe.

Difficult Decisions

There were particularly difficult decisions during these days. Would we allow an order to not revive her should she stop breathing? Would we sign an "Expectancy of Death" form so we would not be bombarded with questions when she did go?

These were bizarre, and painful decisions to be a part of. We were trying to focus on helping her to live...not die. Others seemed to be focused on her impending death. Necessary and painful, but this was part of the process.

Then came her last day with us. She weighed in at 5 pounds! We were thrilled. She failed a bit in the afternoon, struggling to breathe and then rallied up with all her strength that evening. We didn't know but she was preparing for her greatest journey ever... her trip home to heaven. She was so active all night.

Good-bye Our Precious One...
At about 5 in the morning, I sensed an inner call to go and be with our son, Brendyn. This had not happened as strongly as this before. Her Daddy came and took over the vigil. I gave Jayde to Dale to hold and they both fell asleep upright on the couch.

Strangely unknown to him at the time it gave him a chance to hold his precious Daughter just one last time. He loved her so deeply and she him...this precious bond between Daughter and Daddy. One last perfect picture of Daddy and Daughter.

A few minutes later I came by to check on her and without either of our knowledge, she had stopped breathing... She was gone...just as they predicted she would go.

THE OCEAN JOURNEY

Standing on the ocean shore...
I wave goodbye to you, my precious one
I watch you sail away...
Further, further from my site,
until you're out of view.
I find myself wondering how I will ever,
ever live through this so intense a storm,
of so final a goodbye.
Goodbye my precious, I whisper in the night.
That seems to fall upon deaf ears.
Please don't leave me here alone.
I may just fall apart.

I am not sure of what is now before me
I now sail alone without you,
floundering in my deepest ocean grief.

PAUSING FOR REFLECTION

Death begins to stare us in the face the moment we either hear that someone has gone, or when we get the news, usually from doctor, that the end is imminent. From that moment on we begin to grieve. We struggle with the news. We move from our denial to our hope and back to our denial again. We often begin to pray, in desperation for a miracle.

Painful Reality - What Now?
We don't want to step into the next days and months but we find ourselves wading into the cold waters of our pain. We wade in just a bit and then out, in, and then, out again. Soon we find ourselves wading in deeper and deeper accepting more and more of the realities we are faced with.

Wading Deeper in the Cold Waters
We hold our loved one close and sometimes find the holding, too scary. We are on sacred ground in these last moments.

The time just before our loved one dies becomes so precious in our memories. Whether we know that the end is near or are surprised by that wicked blow of death, those moments are precious. We struggle to remember, to savour.

Standing on Sacred Ground

We imagine and somehow know that our loved one was saying goodbye in some important way. For some, those are beautiful memories. For some, they are filled with the pain of watching someone suffer. For others, harsh words were said on the way out the door followed by a fatal accident or heart attack.

My friend on his deathbed wasn't really himself; as the medication he was on took us from him long before he actually left us. Good-byes felt inadequate.

Imperfect Last Good-byes

No matter what the circumstance, these are sacred and often very imperfect moments. Not always as we wish they could have been. We as humans struggle to make sense of them.

We struggle with the guilt of not saying the right thing. We struggle with the pains of saying the mean words. We struggle with needing to connect through those moments and sometimes feeling robbed of precious last moments alone.

Some parents wish they hadn't given that child the keys to the car or let them go out that night.

We tussle with what it all means for us. We try to make sense of it, but no sense can be made.

We muddle through all of this sometimes for weeks as if it might help us feel better or even bring them back somehow. In the end, we are left with the harsh reality.

Our precious one has left us, with all these confusing and painful feelings and no way to fix them. We may try to fix them or reason them away but it doesn't work. This is our reality. This is the way it is. It isn't changing.

Struggling to Make Sense of it All
Somehow we find a way to make sense of it in our hearts. Somehow our head finds a way to calm our hearts. Somehow we make peace with these final moments, each in our own way. After all they are final and we cannot change the past.

The moment for goodbyes has past and we are left with just how it was.

Did I Do Enough?
For me, as an exhausted mother, who was pumping milk many times a day for Jayde, I struggled with the questions. Did I let myself bond enough with her? Did I hold back because she would hurt me? Did I fight for her enough with the

doctors who were convinced that she would not live anyway? Did I give her enough love? The questions went on and on.

That last afternoon with us, an aid had been brought in to hold her and give me a break; a chance for me to get some things around the house done. Oh how I regret not just holding her that afternoon... savouring every moment. She had been doing so well that I did not expect this to be her last day with us.

We do the Best We Can with What We Have
In the end I knew, I had to believe that I had done the best I could, with the strength I had at the time. She knew she was loved and wanted. What more could a little one want? Yet it was never enough for me.

As a parent the struggle is often - Did I do enough? What did I miss? Should we have fought harder with the medical experts for her life? Should we have? Should we have? Should we have? The questions rang in my ears.

Sometimes you can make yourself crazy with the things that go through your head during this time. It is so very difficult to know what to do with these thoughts and feelings.

Just Be
Yet, it is important to just be honest with what we feel. We need to share it with someone, to get it off our chest as many times as needed.

It is important to release ourselves from the expectations that we have to do this "death thing" perfectly. Life is not perfect. Why should death be perfect, or even our goodbyes. In the end we are human; death and life are all part of that humanity.

Life is not Perfect...Death is not Perfect
Eventually, we forgive ourselves and grant ourselves the grace to say, "It is what it is and it was what it was." Then in whatever time we need, it becomes time to release ourselves of these thoughts, guilty feelings and let go. This too takes time, as well as internal and external processing which is not an overnight process.

Please do not for a minute think that I am suggesting that this is easy. Even now I find myself traveling back to those final moments the day before and wishing I could have done something better or differently. I have heard of others who struggle with this for years after the final goodbye. They wonder what could they have done differently or said in a better way.

It is What It is

In the end I am forced to come back to the same place. It is what it is, imperfect and yet full of beautiful memories. And now the hardest work of all begins...

Bon Voyage...
Bon Voyage...

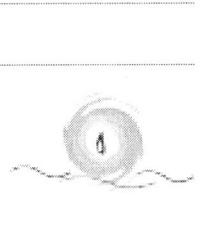

Chapter 1

Chapter 2

Shipwrecked

"The Tearing, Wrenching Few Moments and Days Just After..."

Gone... just gone... just like that...

I am, tossed into the icy, merciless ocean
I cannot breathe...
The ripping and tearing...
too great to bear...

I fear I will drown... I fear I won't drown
I fear...

Fragmenting...into many painful pieces....
My soul cries out to hold you...
to be held... just once more.
That would be enough...
NO it will never be enough

A nightmare, unfolding
before my very eyes...
No... in my soul... my broken soul
My empty...broken broken soul

The deep, deep ocean of my grief.

SHARING OUR STORY

Our world is in a moment tossed headlong into the raging waters. We are being shipwrecked by the worst storm we had ever faced... At first we just go through the motions.

Angry Storm Rolls In
I am dialing 911. I am thinking, "Is this really the end?" Ambulance. A drastic, desperate effort to save her. A futile yet desperate ambulance ride - when I looked into the driver's eyes, we speak silent words of knowing. The doctor's words, "It's no use. She's gone." He seems to know. Another person speaks the empty words, "You knew this would happen!"- as if that was supposed to help.

Final Precious Moments
We find ourselves sitting there holding our dear, precious, beautiful and perfect little Jayde. Her body now cold. No life left. We hold and hold and hold and cry. Dear friends cry with us. We stroke her soft cheek, and hold her tiny hands one last time.

Weeping and holding and saying goodbye to this precious body and soul who had wormed her way deep into our hearts. The beginning of so many

Shipwrecked: The Tearing, Wrenching Few Moments & Days Just After

goodbyes. The beginning of the worst day of my entire life.

How ironic, it was her best day. The day with no oxygen tank or tube in her nose... at peace in her Heavenly Father's arms. Yet for Dale and I... the worst. Then they came. They took her from my arms. They actually took her from us... and I released her body to them.

Just like that, I would never lay eyes on her on this earth again. That night I was cuddling her until morning, and now, my arms will never feel her again.

Shipwrecked... Tossed into the Vast Seas
My mother soul and Dale's daddy heart are tossed into the vast seas. There is a ripping. We have been shipwrecked, in the cold dark waters, of loss. Left alone now. Only thing left is to phone people. Tell them the news, that cold dark news. Only weeks ago we had shared the news of her birth. Now we tell of her passing. I'd really rather not.

Not Real - Yet Way Too Real
We walk out of the hospital, empty, cold, alone. A cloud hangs over our souls. The whole world turns grey. We find ourselves at our dear friend's home, unable to go home to the emptiness just

yet. We are in a vacuum, or in a cloud, everything is hazy - not real - yet way too real.

We try to help our 5-year-old son to say goodbye too. Not having thought this part of the process through, we do what we can. How does one do this well? He doesn't seem to understand...or maybe he understands better than all of us?

Too Much, Too Bare
Friends come...all I can do is curl up and weep, wrapped in a blanket. I am so cold - right to the core of my being. So much love trying to reach me. It barely gets into my soul. It does; but I can hardly feel it. The love is holding me together...just like my blanket. People say, "eat". Food nauseates me. I am drowning in my soul. My arms are empty and that is all that matters.

How Will I Do This?
Dreams are gone. How can I ever live again??? I keep thinking that. How will I do this? I am pretty sure I cannot; yet some part of my soul keeps on breathing. At one point I go into the bathroom, just curl up in a ball and weep. I need a smaller room. It might hold me together or it might help me hold myself together. It doesn't seem to help.

Nothing helps. This is a nightmare that I fear I just may not survive. The smaller space feels safer

Shipwrecked: The Tearing, Wrenching Few Moments & Days Just After

somehow. I am swallowed up by the hugeness of it all. Dale, meanwhile is drowning in his own corner - coping in his own way - his Daddy heart broken.

Finally we force ourselves to go home. The place is empty. Her cradle sits in the corner just as we left it. We don't know what to do now. Is this the life we are left to live? Exhausted we go to bed, to a fitful sleep; awaking to the nightmare of our new reality. This is the nightmare we will awake to for many mornings. But, this first morning is the worst. This is our new stark reality.

Void! Empty Cradle... Empty Arms... Empty Heart
I wake. She is not beside me as she was for so long. Her empty crib next to my bed; I long for her. Why do we even get up? But we do. We put one foot in front of the other like we will for so many a morning... with no life or purpose. Today we must, for we have a meeting at the funeral home.

I feel as though I am walking in a dreamworld. Is this really us? We sit at a big fancy table. If her leaving isn't enough, reality forces us to hurry up and decide things. Cremation? Burial? Casket? Service? Then comes the money talk. They are kind and business-like. They talk money, service folders and boxes to put her in.

Chapter 2

Only half listening, I remember having a different conversation in my head, "I am being asked to pay money for something that I didn't choose. I didn't choose her death! I have no money for this! I have no desire to bury my precious little baby!! I don't want to pay money for something that I don't even want to do!" I am suddenly aware... they have her here somewhere. Where is she?

I Didn't Choose This!
In the end we choose. We decide on the little wooden box. Dale wants the real wood. So wood it is; it is a good choice. We are numb by now. It's too painful. We are so thankful for the two dear pastor friends who sit there and keep us focused.

We resign to the funeral expenses. We don't care. Jayde is our precious little one and she has been ripped from us. The rest doesn't seem to matter. I just want her back. "Let's just get out of here!"

The people at the funeral home have been kind. They would rather not do this either; that is comforting.

Kind and Gentle Connections
We go home. Greeted by our friends who are so present and loving. We often say throughout the process; we are blessed to be so loved.

So we plan her service. This feels strangely good. We feel connected to her somehow as we plan to celebrate her. We plan music and balloons, and symbolism and communion. All our friends pitch in to help - with music and balloons and food and most of all the hugs.

Dreams and Hopes Dashed
The day in between the service and the planning is a calmer one. We are waiting. We have worked so hard to prepare a celebration worthy of such a precious beautiful daughter.

This is the only celebration we will plan for her. There will be no graduation. There will be no wedding. There will be no confirmation. There will be no nothing (or so we thought). We cry for all the never haves and for all the never will haves. We have done the best we can for her. Now, we are ready to bring her to the church for the first time and the last time.

We have talked. We have decided that somehow, we will not allow ourselves to die with her. This is all we know for now. Although we have no idea how to even go about that. She would not want us to quit living.

We will take what she has taught us and be ever present to every moment, for the rest of our lives.

Chapter 2

We will share what she has given us with others. This is noble. Still, our souls are devastated but we will eventually choose life. For now... we just hurt!!!

Intense Lull in the Storm
I will never forget that quiet Sunday in between the planning and the service. All is so deadly still. People are not around. We are alone in our pain. There is such an intense lull in that deadly storm. We are not talking to each other much. Our pain is too big to share and hearing the pain of the other is too much.

I walk into the living room where her cradle still is. I will never forget the painful picture that awaited me. Daddy is sitting in the rocking chair where he rocked his precious little girl. He is holding her bonnet next to his cheek; he is weeping and sobbing. She has broken his heart (I don't think he ever really believed that she would really go).

His pain frightens me. I weep for him... for me... and I run to the phone. I cannot handle this part of this death business... not yet. I need help and quickly. I call a pastor friend to come and be with him. He comes. It helps. Such a picture of love; beauty and horror all wrapped into one bit of time.

For Now We Just Hurt!

My dear friend, who stands close beside me, takes me shopping for a dress for the funeral. She says I need one and so I go. Later, on the day of the funeral I will be glad I did. I find something. The lady in the store asks what the occasion is. I answer rather matter-of-factly, that it is for my daughter's funeral. (I shake my head... Did I just say that?)

It is still so unreal. It echoes in my ears. I do not even ask the price of the dress or of the necklace. I pull out my credit card. I sign it. I look. It is $250 dollars. I don't care. I have something to wear and that is that. It is over.

Sacred Day

The day of her funeral comes. We prefer to call it her celebration. It softens the blow. It goes as beautifully as a funeral can. All to soon, we find ourselves at the graveyard... to bury the body of our precious babe.

It is hardly real... yet so real. The hole is dug. They put a nice green carpet around it to stand on, and to make it less awful. It doesn't work. It is still awful. We say things. The pastor says things. I think we sing, I can hardly remember. I am numb.

Dale puts her little box in the ground. In a moment that is long for him, he makes sure it is firm, solid and safe (he tells me later). Her cousin gently places a special, small, soft pillow on the top of that precious little box. She has made it as her special gift to Jayde and it gifts us too.

The children have balloons and they let them go. Up. Up. Up. Up! It is profound and beautiful - so right and so wrong all at once. I am numb. Through this whole thing... I cannot seem to cry for some reason. Certainly not because I have no feelings - just too many people... too much to feel. I must get through this day - survive it - I cry later.

One Breath at a Time
It is a better day for us; it helps us feel closer to her - almost like she is still with us. The kids wave ribbons, flags and sing, "Jesus loves me". Lots of music. Lots of love. Our pastor friend talks of breathing. She lived life like this; breathing moment by moment into the next. We will too. It helps.

She breathed her way into eternity. We must now breathe our way through the next days...one breath at a time. I can do that. I can breathe one breath at a time, but for today, that is all I can do. People come - lots of hugs and I'm sorry's. We are not alone.

Then, we are alone; it is all over. Our last connection to her feels gone (later we find other ways for connection; but this important one is over and she seems to leave with it). We find ourselves sitting in our living room. There is no cradle in the corner - there is no little Jayde to hold.

We have food. We have balloons. We have flowers. We don't have the only thing we want; to touch and cuddle our little Jayde Mikayla... our little gem.

We are Alone - It is Over
We are too tired to cry; we go to bed in exhaustion. We have been tossed into the uncharted and very frightening waters of deep grief. They have been sailed by others before; but to us they feel like a deep dark hole. Breathe. Sleep comes to provide escape from our painful reality.

Tomorrow we will wake to yet one more empty day without her - one more nightmare that is real - as each sun rises. Yet for now we can escape.

THE OCEAN JOURNEY

The storm has come;
unexpected, harsh, inescapable and unforgiving.
Our boat until now... solid, secure,
large enough to handle anything.
Now... it feels so small...so vulnerable.
The sea so very large.
Waves roll over,
numb one minute,
intense the next.
Tossed, shocked, cold.
Suddenly the ocean is bigger than life itself.
Suddenly the water beneath
is turbulent and frightening.
This ocean deep seems
to have swallowed up my loved one;
and now it threatens to swallow me.
How deep.
How wide.
How overwhelming this goodbye,
This deep deep ocean of my grief.

PAUSING FOR REFLECTION

Reflecting on this part of our journey, I find myself saying, "Who would want to hear this painful story...what am I doing sharing this?" Then I remember how I longed for people to really understand the craziness we found ourselves in. How I loved to be with people who just understood at a deep level, my feelings. So I push past these worries to share this with you. If it helps only one soul, that is enough for me.

So You May Feel Understood
This part of the journey is a place where everything is everywhere. It is the most intense time of all. Everything feels so very final. There is an intense tearing of the soul as the loved one is literally ripped from our presence. Emotions run rampant and change from second to second. Numbness is common; so is intense feeling. People move back and forth between the two.

The word, "final" came to my mind very often. I just wanted this to be different so badly but felt so helpless and the helplessness made me angry. I felt forced to do things (like burying her) that I really didn't want to do. Some parts of me felt sorry for myself, so I moved to the place of pity and being victim. I didn't care what people thought, which was quite refreshing. I just wanted the pain to end.

Desperate Thoughts Invade
During this time, people often flock to help and I thank God that they do. Without them one would not get through. At the same time, the love that is shared is often not really felt until later, when reflecting. At the time it is hard to deeply feel their presence. It is a numbing time, in order to protect ourselves from going crazy, therefore it is hard to let it all in.

Many thoughts invade the mind during these days. They are often desperate thoughts. My friend said to me, "I am thirty some years old and my life is over." Of course that wasn't true, but for her in that moment it was true.

Some people say words like "Why and Why us and What if?", over and over and over. I remember repeating to myself, "It's so final...It is so final." There are also thoughts like we had, of wanting to really honour that person. There are thoughts of wanting others to honour them too and know just how incredible that person was. Some shut off their feelings and just move into the "doing" of a proper burial.

Intense Empty Spaces

The physical "gone-ness" of that loved one is so intense that it is hard to know what to do with that physical void. We are physical beings, therefore are devastated when the physical is ripped from us with no choice. Husbands and wives go to bed holding pillows or stuffed animals just to fall asleep. Mothers hold the blanket of that little one in desperation, just to fill the emptiness.

Parents ache to tuck that little one in just one more night. Wives and husbands move to a different bed or fill the empty side with pillows. In spite of all our attempts to fill the emptiness, there is the empty silence and physical reminders of their presence just moments or days ago. Our efforts seem to serve as futile reminders of their absence.

No Right Way - Grief Follows No Rules

The ones left behind are barely surviving. Some feel deeply in these days. Others are numb. Most are doing quite a bit of both. Grief brings no rules. People are feeling deeply, sometimes so deeply that they cannot stand to feel anymore.

My dear friend who lost her husband years ago had to be medicated through his whole funeral just to get through. Some have to go to the funeral in wheelchairs, so they don't faint. One does whatever it takes to just get through. There is no right way; there is no wrong. It is just is what it is.

Most are Barely Doing What They're Doing
These are bitter and tearing days. Sometimes only the presence, love and prayers of others can make it bearable. Even breathing feels like a task. One struggles to make sense of the pain and sometimes to fix the "unfix-able". People feel like they are going crazy. Some get suicidal thoughts. The days get long and the nights get longer. Most are barely doing what they are doing.

This is a time in the process for those around a person who is grieving, to be the most present. It can be tempting to be afraid to sit with someone when they are feeling such deep emotion. We are just not used to that. Yet during this intense storm in the soul it is important to stay present and encourage people to lean into their intense pain.

Stay Present... Dare To Be
Dare to just BE with them in it and do not try to fix it for them or to leave them because of your discomfort. Just hug or cry with them or even just sit with them. Let them do what they need to do. There are no rules. Follow their lead. Not your agenda for what you think they may need. Be

present. No advice. No right answers. No fixing. Another important need is to have people who are thinking straight, walk you through all the preparations that need to be made.

Often in these intense times, those around the people who are grieving are so uncomfortable with feelings that they just try to fix them. From good motivation people sometimes come up with a string of "right answers" that can sometimes be so painful.

For example it may sound comforting to others for God to need our angel more than us; but this just made us angry. We didn't want an angel in heaven - we wanted our angel right here with us. Or a common statement could be, "she is in a better place." The trouble for me was even though that may be true; as a mother, I could not think of a better place for her to be except in my arms.

One Breath at a Time
Usually there are some words that are uttered that just reach into our soul and comfort us. Our pastor's reminder in the sermon, to breathe, was so helpful for us. All we needed to do was to breathe our way to healing...one breath at a time. I could see how I could do that task, sometimes barely, but it was mostly "do-able".

One grieving friend of mine put coloured stickers all over her home just after her husband died to remind her to just breathe.

Let it Unfold

I remember a friend saying to me when I asked her what she needed just days after her husband's sudden death. She said, "breathing is nice". I learned from this to keep the words, simple and to the point.

Another colleague of mine simply reminded us to "Let it unfold.". This was so helpful to me. It freed me from having to figure any of it out. I could just be with the process just as it was in that day. There was nothing to fix; nothing to do. What relief!

Be Gentle With Yourself

If you are reading this in the midst of your grieving process remember to be very gentle with yourself. You may be able to make sense in hindsight of some of your feelings and reactions. Don't judge yourself for them. You are understood. It is a difficult time... the most difficult you will ever likely experience. Hopefully this just helps you to feel understood.

Give yourself room to have grace for yourself during those times. You are not crazy; it just feels crazy. This "crazy-making" experience one usually moves out of as the intensity continues. Remember you are in good company of many who have travelled this road before. Some people tell me that they find themselves thinking that they are just a mess or a wreck. Let me say just one thing to that, "IT IS NORMAL".

Follow Your Heart and Soul to Healing
No matter how you react to this experience, these few days feel like one is being tossed into the ocean with nothing else to do but to tread water. Don't force yourself to comply with a bunch of rules. Just follow what you know; it will heal you.

It is the beginning of one of the most difficult processes any man, woman or child ever has to live through. Notice I say, 'live through". By some amazing miracle, we do get through this intense pain and can move into a fulfilling life again.

The ability for us as human beings to heal is amazing. Although people do not feel as though they will ever smile or be happy again; they find themselves one day still in the land of the living. To their surprise, they are actually loving life again.

But, first comes the process of grieving and healing. This process actually begins the moment our painful reality sets in. Just "breathe" your way into the next moment and trust that, "It will unfold".

/ Shipwrecked: The Tearing, Wrenching
Few Moments & Days Just After

Shipwrecked...
Shipwrecked...

Chapter 2

Chapter 3

Riding The Waves

"An Emotional Roller Coaster"

Feelings.... Deep Intense Feelings
Flooding me...
Bricks on my chest...I cannot breathe

Then moments later.. I feel nothing..
Reprieve from the pain.....

The wave comes.. washes over me...
I cry... I weep
Once again the feelings flooding..

I fear I will drown
I fear I will not drown.
I fear I will never stop crying.. if I start.

The pain... I wake with it... I sleep with it.
The deep, deep ocean of my grief.

Chapter 3

SHARING OUR STORY

The day after we put our precious little one into the ground reality sets in like never before. The tremendous tearing in our souls deepens... this is really real. She is really not coming back. We try to pay bills - to keep busy. I try to hold my feelings in. I am trying to avoid feeling them. However this only makes it worse.

Bricks on My Chest
I feel like bricks are on my chest... I cannot breathe. I literally cannot breathe! I am frightened, until I realize that I need to let it out. Holding on to the pain is making it worse. So I cry – relief, for a moment. It is a catch 22. Crying hurts so much and not crying kills me. I hate this!!! One minute I am fine (whatever that is) and the next I am absolutely lost.

Just Doing Life - Not Living It
I am doing life. I am not living. Dale goes often to the grave, to be close to her, to care for her I think. I cannot go there. Just when I think I am doing ok, something reminds me. Waves of feelings wash over me and I am once again drowning.

I see the women around me who are pregnant with healthy babies. I have not yet carried a completely healthy baby; I do not want them to have this pain. I just feel that life is so unfair sometimes. I remember feeling this same stuff after losing a baby in the womb.

I walk into the middle of a church service - a baby is being baptized at the front. I race out, tears streaming. It just hurts; sending me headlong back into that emotional roller coaster. Three women are there and I literally fall into their arms... sobbing. They do the best they can to just hear the pain. I am glad for their presence.

Triggers Everywhere
At one point in a restaurant, while out with our friends for supper, only about a week after she is gone; a lady comes in carrying a baby. A baby the size of Jayde, so tiny, so perfect, so healthy, even has the same colour of hair as our Jayde. She cries through the whole meal.

I try once again to hold in the pain, for the sake of our meal. The waves come in. I race for the washroom and burst into tears - I hate this! I hate this! I tell my friend who has followed me, "I just want to die!!" Then the moment is over; the waters are still again.

Chapter 3

We are driving in our van. The three of us. We are so painfully aware that one of us is missing. Will we ever feel whole again!!! I ache when I look back beside our Brendyn and see her sitting there, in that painfully empty chair. We planned for that. Can we not do anything that is not empty? I cry - another wave.

Empty, Empty Void
Going to a movie or two, we take our son. I remember one - a children's show. We are there with our son, and all the other families with children. Jayde is not there with us. We had dreamed of taking her to these fun things. We had dreamed of doing things as a family.

Instead it seems like everyone else is with their families; while we are glaringly missing our daughter. Again we stare directly into the gaping, empty hole of her death. I ache inside. This void, I cannot seem to fill.

My insides are raw. I hug her picture. How futile; yet it works. The ocean is not washing over me any more. It is inside my soul - tossing me about mercilessly. My body is grieving. I am a new mom. My arms ache; my breasts are full and leaking. My hopes and dreams for our family are gone. I am so very, very empty.

Ocean Rages Within

Sometimes when I hold our son, I think of holding her. Sometimes I think I hold him too tightly for fear of losing him too. He reminds me of her. He reminds me of her presence. He reminds me of her absence. I tuck him in at night, saying to him, "I love you". To the heavens, I say, " I love you", in hopes she will hear it.

I ache to watch my family ache. I hate crying. It hurts too much. Imagine - crying hurting more than not crying! But then not crying starts to suffocate me again. This is one huge nightmare. The waters are dark and cold and endless. I fear I will never find dry land.

We try to keep busy; we go shopping. We visit people. We travel. We do anything just to survive and in the end, the ocean of feelings swallows us up again.

Wave after Wave after Wave

Every so often I go to her things carefully stored in her dresser. I take out her clothes. I smell them; even smelling brings out the pain. I hold them close. I find myself crumbling to the floor... holding her clothes and sobbing. Yet another wave. I am learning if I release the tears, I will find some relief, so in desperation I cry. I am tired of crying, of just breathing my way into each moment, but it is all I can do.

As the waves wash over, and over, and over me, I feel more and more alone. The phone is silent during the day. Dale is at work and I am here. I don't say much to him about my pain and he doesn't say much to me.

We find ourselves more alone in our own separate worlds than ever. We don't seem to want to bring it up to each other - almost to protect the other from the pain. Sometimes to avoid hearing of their pain too. It all seems so big and we are almost drowning.

Breathe
I know from my work with others, that this will pass; this intense ocean of pain. My heart cannot believe it. So I breathe. It seems I am attacked by feelings; I honour my feelings. I grieve purposefully and deeply, and the waves come and go; come and go. As the months go on I find the waves are not as frightening. The waters seem a bit calmer. I am healing. What a relief. It is unfolding.

THE OCEAN JOURNEY

The waves roll in.
They threaten to capsize my boat,
which now feels smaller than ever;
in the midst of the vast ocean of my grief.
One moment I am almost fine
(whatever that means).
The next I am washed over
by immense waves of huge emotion.
My feelings
seem to just come and go with the wind.
There is no reason with their coming
and no timing with their going.
My tears mingle with the ocean waves.
At first they frighten me until I realize
that I survive each burst of wave,
that washes over me without my notice,
and leaves me in their wake.
Shaking...crying...feeling...
the immensity of the deep deep ocean of my grief.

PAUSING FOR REFLECTION

It goes without saying that dealing with the overwhelming feelings is the most difficult part of the healing and grieving process. It really does feel like the waves will wash over you and literally drown you. If you really enter into feeling them, you will not be able to turn them off. (Don't worry; you have more control over them than you feel you have. You can turn them off and on.) Many people in this process are afraid of the depths of their feelings.

Surviving Intense Waves

As time goes on, one survives wave after wave. It becomes a comforting fact that one can feel and it is not as overwhelming as first thought. The tears come and go. Oddly enough and almost out of nowhere, some sunny moments appear.

It hardly seems possible that one can feel so good and just when you think, you have the world by the tail; another wave comes and washes over you. **Feeling pain and joy - that bittersweet feeling all mixed together - become a part of one's normal way of being. I am not sure if one befriends the pain or just feels they must do it so they will.**

Relationships are Challenged

Marriages often struggle to thrive during the grieving process. This is often due to the fact that at first the pain shared seems to double it instead of cut it in half. This perception changes over time. The first intense emotions are so hard sometimes to share, due to concern for your spouse or even for one's self.

Dale and I tried to be intentional about moving through our pain. Yet sometimes we weren't very good at sharing our feelings. It is very difficult for spouses to talk with each other about their pain. Sometimes the pain seems almost doubled when shared with someone who is also so deeply living it.

We found it imperative, to find safe places where we could work through some of our grief apart from one another. Through these separate times of grieving, we were better able to journey together.

Enter Deeply into the Healing

In spite of the difficulty with grieving, we had decided that we wanted to choose to heal. The only way to heal, was to enter deeply into it, grieve her fully and allow the healing to unfold. Honouring our feelings in this brought healing because instead of fighting the process, we began to flow with the waters.

We still felt overwhelmed and washed over by waves, but not as afraid. Missing her desperately, we still had to find ways to breathe through each day, learning to trust that if we just allowed ourselves to surf the waves, even going under sometimes without a fight, that we actually came up for air. Each time we were washed under; we came up feeling a bit better, and strangely a bit more anchored.

Riding with the Waves
It may seem like forever, to fight with the ocean of your grief. Yet the best way to be with the tossing of emotions is to allow the waves to move through. Feel them, honour them, and allow them to move. Moving with your grieving process will enable the healing of your soul.

No matter what anyone else thinks, just follow your heart's wisdom. Your grieving heart will know just what to do. Besides, often when you are feeling the most deeply, no one is around. Trust your process. Trust that healing is on its way.

You are in uncharted waters. Your journey is through the painfully cold waters of grief and you need to listen to your soul. So breathe and cry, even sob and wail when you need to. You will move through the waves of pain, minute by minute and day by day.

Moment by Moment
In my experience, every moment was different. Every moment needed something different. When people would ask me how I was; I would sometimes reply, "this moment is ok." or "this moment is not a good one." I knew that my feelings could change from one moment to the next.

Yet, grief has a way of bringing surprises to the moments - some very harsh and painful. Other surprises would gently bring an encouraging ray of bright light.

Trust the Process
We were washed over many times with all kinds of painful emotions and we began to go with it. After all what else could we do with it? We needed to cry. We needed to heal. We felt out of control at times. We were lonely. We were drowning. At times surprisingly, we even noticed ourselves to be living in spite of this turmoil. Thus without our knowing it...we were being brought to healing.

Chapter 3

Riding The Waves...

Chapter 3

Chapter 4

Getting Our Bearings

"Settling Into Our Grieving"

Embracing the journey.

**Painful missing... I hear her voice…
I hope you Dance.**

Healing with intention...

Moving in and out and feeling and breathing and...

**Openings and closings and openings and closings...
Unfoldings.... time to dance.**

Our deep, deep ocean of grief.

Chapter 4

SHARING OUR STORY

Our journey takes a very unusual twist very early on. We begin to sense a call to adopt a child who had no chance for a home. So in the midst of our very deep pain, we decide to open to this possibility. We are not ready for a child to enter our home yet; but we know that an adoption overseas takes months and even years.

So we begin the process of putting paperwork in order. It gives some very regular and important jobs to do each day as we put papers in order. This does not take the place of our pain, but it does help to put order and purpose to it.

Gentle Opening
We realize that if we will open to yet another little one, and open to our dream for family; the time window is very small because of our age. So we begin. We also grieve even more intentionally. It is imperative that we bring a child into a home where we have worked through a good deal of our grieving.

I go for counselling and so does Dale. It is such a relief to talk to this person, as I don't have to protect my feelings from her, as I do Dale nor he me. My intense feelings in her office don't overload Dale because he is somewhere else doing the same thing.

One such session I remember as being so vividly important to my healing process. I was so connected to my grief that I cried for almost three hours. I had a very profound experience in this session.

Sacred Meeting of the Souls
I am invited to go to the place in my body where my pain is and hold it with my hands. I am invited to just close my eyes and be with the pain. She asks me what is there. I reply, "my baby" and I weep as I hold that empty part of me. Then I am panic-stricken. I notice the little baby getting smaller. I say, "she is going" and I weep some more. My spiritual director then suggests that I follow her.

This was a new thought for me. I thought her going meant she was leaving me. So in my imagination, I follow her, and my baby takes me to my feet. She turns about 5 years old down there at my feet. She crawls up on my lap - I stroke her hair and she mine. I weep some more. I tell her I miss her. She asks, "Why? I am right here." I hadn't thought of this before.

Then I am invited to notice if anyone else is there. Jesus is there with us... holding the moment for the both of us. My little Jayde then invites me, "Dance with me mommy." I cry some more and tell her that I cannot. She then wisely says, "Why not? I am right here." So in this sacred place, I dance with her.

Next, I am invited to see if she has anything to show me. She shows me the rest of the world - Children - so many children. I have had enough; I am not ready to see more. I come back from this sacred place. I have cried and cried.

I have had the chance to see that my little one is truly still with me in my heart. In spirit she is truly with God. I have been gifted with an opportunity to weep and to heal. This profound experience has opened me to see a glimpse of the bigger picture.

Don't Grieve What Isn't True
Strangely, after that experience, I feel different. From that time on, I am a bit better. I have flowed a great deal of the ocean in my soul outside of me. My therapist says one thing that is especially helpful for me, "Don't grieve what is not true." She is right. I am grieving everything.

Some of the stuff I am letting myself think about is making it worse. I am grieving that she is gone from me... forever. The truth... I cannot see her or hear her or hold her physical body anymore. That I grieve deeply. But I do not have to grieve that her spirit and soul is dead and gone. In this way she lives. She also lives on, inside of me. In this way, I remember her. She is my daughter and she will always be my daughter.

Painfully, she is not present with me in a physical way, but still very present in all she taught us. Still very present in my memories, she is still very present in my love for her. She is gifting us. She is creating a huge space in our soul to love even more deeply. Room in our soul is slowly being created by her. An opening is beginning for the someday yet to come, beautiful little Haitian daughter that is now only barely possible.

Making Room - More Opening
She is making room for us to think about others who suffer, grieve, and watch their children die of hunger.

She is somehow saying to us..."Dance". Dale used to dance in the living room with his precious little daughter. Now she seemed to be saying to our souls, "Dance with me... Dance with God... Dance

Chapter 4

with life... Don't die too... Just Dance... I am Dancing, so Dance on the ocean waters with me."

Long Lonely Days
I find the days long. Not working, I am home alone a lot. So much time on my hands, I miss her so. People don't call much anymore. They have to work during the day. There are not very many people who are free during the day - I am lonely. I starve for folks who I can talk about my daughter with. I just like to talk about her.

Phone calls from friends and neighbours are so appreciated. They comfort me. Especially the call from my friend who also lost a daughter, and from my friend who had lost her husband. They know. Knowing they know means so much. I try to reach out to people but I don't want to be a pain - I probably am sometimes. I just wish the pain would go away. I am so needy; I am so alone - sigh.

Although we still feel so much pain, we dance, but not without a bit of a fight. A huge part of my soul does not want to hear her voice. I want to be stubborn and I don't want to dance. Shrivelling up in a corner, I want to cry and die. I know this is not possible. Dancing comes in many, many ways, so I will dance. First, I realize, I must choose it.

Angrily Planting Flowers

When summer comes, I realize it is time to plant flowers. I rebel. I don't want to plant flowers! Flowers have no right to live when she is gone. Flowers feel incongruent with how I feel. "Dance...", that still small voice comes again.

So I plant flowers - I am mad - I dig in the dirt, angrily. I plant flowers, I water them, and I find they are pretty. They bring colour to my world. With colour comes some joy, and I find myself dancing, just a bit. Without my permission, my colourful flowers are delighting me.

As I follow my soul, I find myself struggling with what to do with Jayde's room. We never really completely created a full space for her for some reason. However her things were in one room that was to be hers, as she needed it.

Since we have been proposed a child from Haiti (and indeed have accepted this little one into our family) I begin the process of moving things around and making space for another little one. In order to do this I must physically move Jayde's things to a new space. This is very helpful. It forces me to grieve in yet another way.

Making More Space - Opening Wider

So I begin to shuffle dressers around. My son gives up his dresser, which has drawers that are difficult to open, to keep Jayde's things safe. Our son gets a new dresser with drawers that are much easier for him to open. We put the things we are collecting for our little adopted daughter into the dresser that Jayde used to have. It all feels so right. The children sharing... all of them sharing together.

As I move her things around, I cry and sob some more - it is all good. It is all important. After this is accomplished, over quite a period of time, I proceed to clear out the room and paint it for Keysha. Somehow purple is important for her... so purple it is.

The colours give me life. The colours bring out both my grief and my joy. The decorating of a child's room brings out the mix of my pain and my joy. It all seems so right. I am saying goodbye and hello all at once. It is ok. It heals me... as I step into it.

Stepping into Healing Choices

We decide it is time to paint the outside of our house. It is an important part of our process - of our dance. Not really sure why; we are learning that the "why's" really aren't important. We are learning to follow where our soul needs to go. If we follow those inner callings, we learn they bring us to healing.

So we follow. We have come to realize that healing is a choice, not something that happens to us. It is something we choose. We can be victim to this process or we can choose to breathe our way into healing. With our little Jayde calling to us to dance, we choose to heal; we choose life.

THE OCEAN JOURNEY

Up 'til now...
I have felt like my little boat had no oars.
It was tossed about in the ocean deep;
at times at the whim of what came at me.
Then comes a point where I realize;
I do have some choice about where this boat will go.
Yes the ocean is very deep and extremely wide
I find I do have oars after all.
I begin to slowly row...bit by bit,
with intention.
I see the land so far ahead.
The waves still come.
The tears come too.

I find resolve within my soul, to make my way to ocean shore.
I'll ride these waves, I will go through,
and not around this deep deep ocean of my grief.
I choose to allow healing to come in to my grieving healing heart.

PAUSING FOR REFLECTION

Once we settled into our healing process, we came to realize that we were more in charge of it than we thought. We learned how to honour our feelings intentionally. Learning how to trust our process, we also learned what our soul was telling us to do. This happened very gradually for us; we grew into it.

Trusting the Healing Process

Very early in the process we realized that we did not have to be victims to the circumstances in our lives. What a great life lesson for all things that happen. This does not mean that we did not feel anything. On the contrary, I would venture to say that we felt our feeling almost more deeply. We were so intentionally present to our feelings and to what we needed to be whole. As we were more able to talk to one another, our relationship grew.

Stuck in a Grieving Place

It is easy to see why grief becomes so overwhelming for people, that it just takes them out of the game. Sadly, some never get back in. Deep and important relationships get lost in the pain. Precious times with others get lost. Some parents begin to ignore the children they still have because they cannot release the one who is gone. People stay in the place of blaming themselves or their partner for mistakes made. People get stuck somehow. Yet in a strange way this can feel safer than moving into healing.

What a horrible place to find one's self in. In some ways, the "stuckness" and the "not releasing" helps people feel closer to their lost loved one. Yet it disconnects them from those who are living around them.

Sometimes, they have buried their feelings deep within their soul, refusing to feel them. Perhaps they are too afraid to enter into their feelings and as a result they have gone numb. Soon, they do not feel much of anything, anymore. No matter why the "stuckness" began. It becomes a way of coping.

Cope Whatever Way You Can

People cope in whatever way they can. People find themselves doing the strangest things. Some move their papers around or rearrange things. Others move to sleep in another room for a while. It is what it is. We do what we must. Our soul seems to be ordering the movement. I think it is our way of trying to sort out what is happening.

It is almost like an external evidence of what is happening within. Yet it is important to move into these responses; they seem very necessary. With heartfelt certainty, we follow what the soul seems to be asking our body to do. It is an important movement that demonstrates our choice to heal.

Trying to Dance
We had more choices to live than we thought. Does this mean it was easy? No. It meant entering headlong into the pain. The best part is on the other side of the pain. A new, fresh, and even deeper life arises from what we had before we lost her. Although we seemed clumsy as we stepped on each other's toes all of the time; we were trying to dance.

Getting Our Bearings . . .
Getting Our Bearings . . .

Chapter 4

Chapter 5

Harbour Days

"Bittersweet and Special Days"

How do I survive those special days...

Celebrate? Feel?
Ignore? Remember?

I am afraid?
It hurts to recognize them?
It hurts to forget about them?

I find ways... I find my way...

There is no right way...

They come. They go. I breathe.

The deep, deep ocean of our grief.

SHARING OUR STORY

The first holiday we endured without our precious Jayde was a horrible day, only two days after her funeral. The pain was almost unbearable already and this day just doubled it. Valentine's Day!!! We know we want to celebrate our love for each other, our son and yes, even our Jayde.

Painful Tender Times
Celebration is hardly what we want to do. We decide to get creative. It is unknown, where we found the strength or the creativity to come up with this. Death has a way of connecting intimately close to our feelings, therefore intimately close to the creative side of the soul.

Almost numb with our pain, walking about in fog, we go shopping. We buy gifts for all the folks who had helped us celebrate her life at the funeral. Next we deliver the gifts. Somehow, it helps to fill the day and it helps us feel close to her. We have stumbled onto a very important truth, almost by accident. As physical beings we need physical ways to keep her close. This comforts us deeply.

Physical Ways to Feel Close
The next celebration is Easter, celebrating resurrection; expecting to be comforted. In some ways, it is comforting; in another way it feels irrelevant. We have lost our precious daughter and we want her back; not resurrected to be with God.

We have Easter dinner as we always did. I have an idea. On our Easter table, I put a candle that reminds me of her. My soul cries out when I place it there. At the same time it comforts me; brings her closer somehow. After all we were thinking of her absence anyways. As we name it, it comforts us, in a physical way. Now, we light candles at every special occasion.

Go Through the Motions
One day after Easter comes - our son's birthday. Yuck! I do not want to celebrate a birthday! Our grief is so fresh. I go through the motions. He deserves a birthday. Our son is so worth celebrating. So I breathe my way through that day. Making a special cake turns out to be a good distraction.

We invite tons of dear friends. I think we are trying to fill all of the void. It is a way of celebrating the life of the child that is with us. Yet it remains, a hard, hard day.

We both hate celebrating our own birthdays. What parent wants to outlive their child! Wanting her to have birthdays; birthdays were so very hard. We move into celebrating whatever way we can. If we were going to choose life, this was part of it. As hard as it was, it was important for us to step into those days. Stepping in whatever way we needed to, on that day, there were no rules.

Mother's Day was painfully void of my daughter. We sit outside having the first summer picnic in our yard. I longed for all of us to be physically present, painfully aware that my mother heart is not in this day. Gypped of that joy, I listen to my soul.

Time to visit her grave for the first time for me. Her Godmother and I walk there together. A very peaceful and beautiful day, yet painful to the core of my being. I have found a way to be with my daughter and she with me. It is hard to stand by her grave. She is not there. Sigh.

Breathing Through Hard, Hard Days
Advent season creates a deep struggle. The previous year I spent pondering this beautiful new life I carried in my womb. Now she is gone. I miss her so deeply. My insides could burst. I find myself sitting in the living room, in the dark, on the couch, where I used to hold her through the

night, to help her breathe. I remember. I ache... for her.

To make matters worse, I am grieving the void of two daughters. For now we are awaiting the homecoming of a little Haitian child, our newest daughter. Pain is doubled as my mother heart yearns to hold my babies. Void. I pray that our baby might get her papers ready in time for Christmas. That would really help.

Putting up the tree is the hardest. Ornaments I had bought for her and to remember our unborn child are brought out. I breathe and with my breathing comes my tears. Dale puts off putting the lights on the tree. His soul is resisting doing Christmas without her.

Finally he realizes that he has no desire to light up the tree without his baby girl. He remembers the year before, joyfully anticipating her birth while putting up the tree lights. Now - poignantly - pondering her death and how he misses her... sigh... he forges ahead. Christmas is another celebration. Our Brendyn deserves to see the lights too.

Trying to Be in the Void
Christmas is full of void, but also of anticipation, of meeting our new child. No one can ever

Chapter 5

replace our Jayde and the love we feel for her. In spite of ourselves, we have found room in our souls and hearts for yet another child. We are risking love again. It is an important part of our dance.

News breaks. Someone is bringing our Keysha home. Right in the midst of the holidays, she arrives. It is our way of dancing. Jayde is pleased, we are sure about that. Keysha arrives on New Years Eve - A profound message to the both of us to start this year with a new dance.

We feel joy like we have never felt since the day Jayde left us. Our little Jayde is never going to run, play, and laugh with us physically on this earth. Forever this will make us more than a little bit sad. But, we have been called to make space for this little dark-faced, wide-eyed wonder. She comes with a joy beyond comprehension.

Jayde's birthday is a very tough day. What to do. What to do. All four of us go out for dinner. She is not there. Dale spent all day, finding just the right flowers for her grave and getting them perfectly arranged. Daddy needs to do this. He follows his heart; his gift to his baby girl. We breathe through the day, and the day unfolds. Keysha and Brendyn remind us to stay in the dance. Yet, why can't we all be together?

Seasons Wrap Around

The year wraps around and we begin the second year of remembering and of special days. Still painful, yet we know we have found our way through before. It seems we know now to follow our soul's leading. We know now that special days are not days to be forgotten or ignored.

Rather these days are to be felt deeply and yes, even celebrated. Actually, these special days seem to hurt even more. How odd. I thought it would get better. Feeling them more deeply; but they are not taking me out like they did before. A sign of healing, I believe.

THE OCEAN JOURNEY

The impending special days.
Those harbour days,
when my wee boat rests for just one time or two,
and my heart remembers
to the depths of my being.
Your day... Our day... Everybody's day...
A part of me wants
to skip this part of my ocean journey.
It is too painful to remember
and too painful to forget.

It connects me to you in some strange way.

It brings you back into my boat with me

for just a while;

one precious little while.

You are strangely here with me

at the same time as being gone.

It is like I row my boat into the harbour

and you get in for just a bit.

We celebrate and connect

and then you seem to fade...away again.

I hardly know just what to do with these times.

And so I allow myself to be

with the sweet memories of you.

I celebrate you and what we had

and love you close to my soul.

Then I row my boat back out to sea;

out into my healing ocean sea;

my deep deep grieving ocean sea.

PAUSING FOR REFLECTION

Like many we were nearly terrified and even paralysed by the impending special days ahead of us. There is a helplessness and a not knowing of what to do with these days. The anticipation of the pain of those days was worse than when the day came. In a strange way, those days helped us feel connected and close to her. We continue to remember her on special days. She is our daughter. To be with her memory and our love for her, connects us to her, especially on those days.

No Point in Pretending
We learned a very important lesson in experiencing this part of the journey. Our soul seemed to know just what we needed to do or not do. If we followed our soul, we would not be disappointed.

Learning there is no escaping the pain of those days, we faced them head on. There is no point pretending that she wasn't on our minds or try to avoid the absence of her. It was our constant companion, why would a special day be any different. Actually it became even more full of void.

Remembering by others on those days is still very important. It tells us that they know that this is still painful. It will always be painful to some degree; so we feel understood and loved. On Jayde's 2nd birthday, our friends looked after our kids.

We could just go out together on a date and be with the memory of her death. After, we took a cake over to their house and put candles on it. Letting our children blow them out, we remembered her. Smile. Sad? We all missed her. Good? Yes. Important? Yes. Still, oh so very sad, our souls wept.

Creative Ways... Can Heal Us

Far too many people do not do what their heart needs to do. They fear that others may think they are a bit crazy, or judge them for their actions. In grieving, most people don't judge us and if they do; they have no idea.

Do what your heart needs. Listen to your soul. It will tell you how to travel even the most difficult days with creativity and grace. Most of all trust yourself. Do not be afraid to feel the loss; for it is in the feeling of it, we are healed.

Harbour Days . . .
Harbour Days . . .

Chapter 5

Chapter 6

Shipmates

"Our Companions on the Journey"

You walk beside me...
You breathe with me...
You cry with me...
You listen to me...
You hold me and my pain...

I am not alone...
For you are with me...

And God is with me through you....

Healing my soul

In the deep, deep ocean of my grief.

Chapter 6

SHARING OUR STORY

Dale and I often comment on how blessed we are to have people love and care for us through this grieving process. The love and presence of these people is so critical. Without them, we don't know how we would be able to find a way to dance with death and heal. People hold us up when we cannot hold ourselves.

Invited to Be and to Live
The first two weeks after Jayde's death are spent far away, at our dear friend's place. They invite us to come and "Be" in their home. This is the most incredible gift they could have given us. For it is there that we are being held, fed, loved, cried with, and even laughed with, in spite of our pain.

They invite us to go for walks, to the opera, and to all the things that represent life going on. Although we sometimes resist, we go along and begin to live those first days without our child.

These are such painful days, but we are being loved and held. Through them we are invited to continue to put one step in front of the other and live even when we don't want to.

Nurtured and Encouraged to Live
We remember the many times our friends come to pick up our son, so we can just be in our grief alone. The outings give him some fun because I don't think we are doing very well at that. We are barely surviving. We are given the space we need to breath, grieve and enter into our pain.

Deeply Understood
Some friends who lost their teenage son a few years earlier come over, cook us supper, and sit with us. How good it is to talk with and to be with them. I even taste the food. He is a great cook.

We feel so understood, not needing to explain what we are feeling. They really inspire my wishing to write this for you. We are understood at the deepest level possible, by those who travel this road also.

Love is Felt
People do amazing things around the funeral time. The hugs, the food, the tears, the visits, and the help with the funeral are all so important. We are helped to celebrate our daughter and to grieve her deeply in her service.

Gently Held
Our friends who take us to their home right after she died; literally hold our broken hearts together.

God is holding us together through them. We are helped to celebrate our daughter and to grieve her deeply in her service. We are literally held together in loving arms and helped to make decisions, as we could not think straight about what to do next.

Accepted in the Grieving

All those who listen, listen, and listen, not in pity but in compassion; they pull us through. God is listening to us through them. Our souls are heard at the depths of our pain and accepted in the hearing.

Pain is Heard... So is Joy

Family members come to help us sort pictures, make meals, help to pay for funeral expenses, and watch Brenny. We are reminded that we are not alone and very loved.

Not Alone

Several remember special anniversaries and days; making a point of being there for us on those days. When they remember her they remember us. We are once again not forgotten in our grieving.

Remembered in Prayer
There are those who prayed and still pray. We are wisely guided back to a healing place in compassion and through safe places.

Gifted with Guidance
In their wisdom, counsellors guide us to the depths of our grief and out into the dance. Their compassion and love is ever felt.

Shared Experience
My partner and lover, Dale, who is with me, feeling deeply and allowing himself to choose the dance of life with me; his love is ever with me. We dance together the dance of deep soul grief into the dance of living.

Reminder
Our son who continues to remind me that I have to move on, he needs me to live. What a gift.

Profoundly Blessed
We are so deeply and profoundly blessed to be so loved by God, our friends, and by one another. We have been visited by God in our pain.

Chapter 6

THE OCEAN JOURNEY

At times I feel as though
I am the only soul in my boat.
Then my friends swim out to me.
They take an oar and bring a blanket
for my cold and shaking body.
They cry a bit.
They gently hold my body and my soul.
They sit with me and listen
and hold me as I sob from deep within.
They are present in so many different ways.
They do not leave me in the ocean place alone.
So although at times I feel so very alone;
my "Healer" comes in human form,
to hold my deeply grieving soul.
To bring some comfort and company
into my lonely boat.
In human form my "Healer" comes
into my deepest pain.
and loves me close
with love that wells from ocean deep.
Love wider than the ocean,
and deeper than the deepest sea.

PAUSING FOR REFLECTION

I would be amiss in not mentioning that one of the most important parts of getting through a journey like this, is the company. The company of having the healing presence of friends and family. It was so good to experience those who care for us and value us.

Amazingly, people were opening themselves to God, to the possibilities to love even when it was painful to do so. The offering of their company was even more valued, when realizing they also grieve themselves.

Healing Presence of Company
Never underestimate the value of a good support system. We are not meant to be islands in this world. We are created to love and to be loved, to support and to be supported. Thus, we are created to bring the arms of God and of healing to each other.

People Need Each Other
In grief, some people close off to this special love. The healing takes a bit longer. Some are afraid to be vulnerable. Some are afraid of what others think. For some, staying open is too difficult.

However, when we do stay open to the people and the love that surrounds us; their love heals us. This I truly believe. Yet, it is hard to trust; it is so hard to reach out. In grief one already feels so vulnerable. Yet for us it was so worth the risking.

More importantly we were so grateful for the presence of good people around us who are really willing to just "Be". In their support, they did not try to fix our pain; making a journey that feels almost unbearable, something we may just survive.

Daring to Stay Open
Remember to reach out... to the safe people. Be as vulnerable as you dare and let others love you to healing. The easiest choice is to crawl into a hole and hibernate - not letting anyone in. Yet the arms, ears, and hearts of others nearby, bring tremendous healing.

So open to the gift of love that is yours and you will not regret it. You are a gift to them as well, when you do this. Without the love and care of others, I would not have found the strength to heal... let alone dance.

Remember, most of the time people want to be there for people when they hurt. They just don't know how.

The Healing of Gentle Presence
For those of you who have friends who are grieving and are not sure how to be there for them; stay with their process. Your presence is so needed. It is going to be a long haul and it is made so very much easier if you are willing to stick by them.

Remember to check in with them regularly. Remember to ask them what they need - never assume. Be present to their pain and their needs. Help them to get out and re-enter life as they are ready. Sometimes it might be appropriate to encourage their participation even when they resist and are not ready.

Just do everything with gentleness. They are so hurting and so vulnerable. Honour their process.

You Will Be Gifted
The neatest thing about being willing to travel this journey with someone who is in this pain is that you will also be gifted in the process. I know this because I have travelled this journey with many.

When you enter into pain so deeply, you are being ushered into a very vulnerable place. This is the place where the souls of human beings can meet at the deepest level.

Chapter 6

I know that the friends who walked this road with me are still fast friends. Our friendship is much deeper than when we began this process together.

Tender Loving "Holdings"

There are times when one just wishes that God would literally come down in the flesh and hug us and tell us that we are going to be ok. and that we are going to survive. Yet in a very real way, God does do this for us through the tender loving "holdings" brought through other people.

I find this to be a profound reality both when I am the one receiving the care and the one giving it. Allow yourself to be hugged in this way both by people and through them by your maker whose love goes beyond the deepest ocean or the widest seas.

Shipmates . . .
Shipmates . . .

Chapter 6

Chapter 7

Finding Dry Land

"Living with Death"

I can hardly believe I have survived
this deeply painful journey...

No. Better yet...I am living it.

I feel so many emotions... none so intense
I feel guilty... for being happy...
Breathing deeply... smiling sometimes...
crying sometimes...

This is life. The mix of joy and sorrow.
It is rich... I can dance... in both.

My healing is unfolding... as it always will
I can enter the dance of life.

I no longer feel like
I am in the deep, deep ocean of my grief.

SHARING OUR STORY

I am not quite sure when our process moved from surviving to living. It is different now. Such a long time ago, it seems that I found myself in a very painful process.

Out of the Fog
Coming out of a fog, things look much clearer now. I am grateful for the life I have been given. Being grateful for the gift of our baby daughter, I ponder all she has taught us in this pain. Somehow I am even grateful for the life lessons in the pain.

I can talk of her now without crying. Her special days can be celebrated without being so frightened of them. Strangely, they are more painful the second time around. Not being quite as numb, I feel things more deeply.

Enough healing has happened that I know how to be in my pain. My pain doesn't make me as afraid anymore. Pain hasn't taken me out yet, so I doubt that it will now. I feel stronger. Looking at her picture, I feel a huge deep sigh coming to my soul. She was so perfect and so beautiful. I go to my sadness, but that is ok.

Finding Dry Land: Living with Death

Pain is No Longer as Frightening
We take a family picture. She is not in it. Yet she belongs there too. I long for her siblings to know her. One day they will. Daddy shows them her picture and tells them about her. They seem to like this. They seem to know. I am glad but still sad.

Visiting the cemetery as a family, the kids play around the graves. The sun shines. We know we are blessed, but this is a sad place, yet a peaceful place. Her place is not here. She is not here. Yet this is where we put her body, so we go there to feel close.

Keysha catches my eye. She is very close to the age Jayde would have been. I long to see Jayde dancing, singing, laughing, and sleeping so peacefully. Strangely enough, God chose to send us a child with great rhythm and a natural ability to dance. Nothing comes by accident it seems.

Holding my children so dear, they are more precious now because I know how fragile life is. I go into their rooms when they sleep, just to watch them and smile; sometimes, finding myself afraid of losing them too. I catch myself checking to make sure they are breathing when they sleep. How foolish it seems, but I have lost big and cannot bear the thought of losing like this again. Sometimes fear just rules. Scars.

Choose to Dance - Amid the Pain
Other times I find myself feeling so incredibly blessed to have this beautiful family that I hold so dear. Being so blessed to have experienced the richness of losing someone and learning how to not live as a victim in the pain. I have chosen to dance... amidst the pain. Alone, I could not have done that.

I Don't Just Know - I KNOW
In my office, I journey with others in their grieving process. I am glad to be with them - although it is sometimes painful to hear of the loss of others. With a new sensitivity, I don't just know...I KNOW. It seems they know I know. This is a gift. The choice before me is to allow it to gift others or take myself out of the dance. I choose to dance.

How strange it is to have such a mix of joy and sorrow all packed into one life. Then I realize this is how life is. It is never just one or the other. We now have a void in our home, an empty chair. One less child at Christmas to buy presents for. On and on, this is never going away. Instead of filling the void in, I shall let it stay. It will help me to be honest and open. I will choose to dance amid the void.

Finding Dry Land: Living with Death

Embracing the Void

On my grandmother's old antique table I have three pictures. One of our family as it is now, one of Jayde alone, and one with Brendyn and Keysha. This is what it is. This is our family, beautiful and missing. We must hold all of this in one lifetime.

This will never be any different. However, I do not hurt as I did before. Still, I long to see my baby girl and to hold her. Looking back I see her with joy and pain mixed. So is our dance - joy and sorrow, life and death; letting it unfold.

We have found ways to remember her. Ways to keep her close in a physical way. For some reason that is important for me. I wear her little locket around my neck, where I can touch it anytime. It helps me to feel her close sometimes.

We have a vase that held flowers at her funeral. We often fill it with flowers, especially on special occasions, in memory. Sometimes I even fill it for her Daddy on his birthday or Father's day as a reminder of her.

Joy and Sorrow Mixed

In my flower garden is a stone with a dragonfly on it, which I put there for her. There are so many physical ways we have found to be close to her...to remember her. These ways comfort us and make us smile. Sometimes they make us feel sad. Both are good. Both are important.

We realize that our life is full of love and the incredible dualism of joy and sorrow - of living with Death. We are choosing to live. We are choosing to dance, even in her absence.

THE OCEAN JOURNEY

I can hardly believe that I can feel so good.
I thought I would be miserable forever,
living on this earth without you.
The intense pain and massive emotions.
The waves. My lonely lonely boat.
My harbour days... so painful harbour days.
My little little boat midst hugest ocean floor;
without an oar it seemed.
Those days when night seemed to mush into day.
I wondered why I put one step before the other.
I am so surprised that not only do I feel ok;
my steps have turned into a dance.
How did this healing happen?
When did it come to me?

But now I see... that it was coming all along.
I was being healed
from the moment my dear little one left me.
I was being healed every lousy excruciating day.
With every tear. With every wave.
With every painful breath from my small boat.
My "Healer" was teaching me
the steps of this new dance,
within the ocean of my grief,
where I now dance in void of you,
yet with fullness in my soul.

PAUSING FOR REFLECTION

In this long process, realizations come to mind regarding those first days. Hardly believing that I would heal and feel joy again let alone survive the experience at all. Also, I realize that getting to this place was a choice. Willingness was needed to step into my pain deeply and feel it as fully as I could in that moment.

Healing is Happening
Trusting my process, I needed to become open to the dance of living again. Every part of my being wanted to lie down beside her and die too. Every

bone in my body rebelled against this dance. My ocean was too deep... my pain too vast.

To Feel Deeply is to Be Fully Alive

Feeling deeply is an integral part of being fully alive and of healing. Those who step into their pain will find life at the bottom of that deep dark ocean. That is the point. Waves keep washing over us in order for healing to really take place at a deep level.

We need to go to the bottom of our pain, to the bottom of our ocean. Just when we think we cannot take another moment we find ourselves not just coming up for air, but rather... swimming ourselves to shore and to our newfound life.

Breath by Breath

Grief has a way of changing people. It either makes us richer and stronger or it finishes us. The really good news is that we can choose if we really believe that there is healing for all this pain. Even when we don't think we can stand it, we can choose to take the next breath.

Really that is all we need to do in order to choose life. For a long time at the beginning, that was all I seemed to be able to do. Just breathe and that was enough.

So we breathe into our pain. We feel it fully, hold it honestly, honour it and allow it to heal. This is simply how we choose to be open to the healing. This is how we can choose to dance in the face of death. All we need to do is Be in our process and trust it.

Step Back to Life
The interesting thing about loss and death, is that is changes you from the inside out. It actually turns you inside out and when you turn yourself back, you are forever changed. The difference can be a change for the good or a change for the worse. The only difference is what I (the person hurting) do with the situation I find myself faced with.

Either I literally grieve forever and die a slow death inside. Or I eventually at the right time in the grieving process choose to re-adjust my thinking so that my feelings follow and bring me back to life.

It is important to note, this does not mean skipping over the important feelings that need to be felt. Both are choices and both happen gradually. One is just more life giving - that is all.

We have not done this "death and grief thing" perfectly. In fact, there is no perfect way. It just is what it is. We have stumbled our way along, struggling to find our way through, the dark tunnels. Sometimes we have had to just go blindly and feel desperately what we felt; trusting that somehow we were going to find our way into a better place. I found this comforting.

Moment by Moment
At some point in our process we became aware that we needed to choose life. So we stepped into the grieving process often with fumbling and bumbling steps, not really knowing what the next step would bring us. Somehow as we stepped into that next moment, the process unfolded before us and we knew where to go next.

As we trusted the process and continued to stumble our way back to life, we found our steps lighter. After what seemed like a very long, long, long, painful process, we found our steps had turned into dancing.

Sometimes we danced even when our hearts were not in it one little bit. I remember being invited to a dance and dinner. We did enjoy ourselves and even danced together.

At the same time our hearts were aching in every breath for our little girl. Sigh... even the remembering of that brings back pain. I think the important thing in this dance was not that we felt like dancing, only that we chose to dance.

Even though we could not even begin to see it at the time, our hearts eventually caught up. What a contrast to the wedding dances we attended this summer... where our tender hearts had healed and we could once again join in the fun with both heart and step.

The Pain Transforms
My experience is that we do heal. Reasons are found to smile again - finding ways to open to life like we could never have thought possible. On that first day, I could never have believed this. Though some part of me knew that I would heal. We do miss our loved one forever. Only the pain changes, that is all.

We will always live with our grief to some degree. However, that is not all there is.

Are we over our daughter??? Of course not. People just don't GET OVER a precious loved one like we would a good movie or the loss of a job or a favourite shirt. Rather I think people re-adjust. Yes, that is what we have done. We have had to re-adjust how we view our life.

We have had to make room in our life for the imperfection of tragedy and change. Things are not as we had planned for our life. But they are good.

Making Room for Imperfection

Yes, I would love to have Jayde back here, so, so much. What would she look like now, I wonder. With great yearning, I would love to see her laugh, play with her siblings, dance with her Daddy, and cuddle with me. In her absence, I know I am living well until the day I see her again. I am going to continue to choose to dance. May you find the strength to do so too.

To Die or To Dance

"To die or to dance"...is the choice we felt we were being given. We really did not know how to dance in the midst of this void. We only knew that we didn't feel much like living. So our God-given soul called us into healing.

Really if you would have asked me what healing looked like I am not sure I could have told you in the beginning. I was in so much pain I was not sure I could see my way to any type of healing - especially not in the first days.

Choose to Heal

Now I know that it is a slow resurrection of myself back to living fully again. I do believe that any of us can choose to enter into this healing. It is an individual process for each of us. Dale's healing was a bit different than mine. I healed differently than my friend. Yet common to all of us is the choice.

We are called to choose to step into this healing; following our maker of our soul back to life and healing.

First it is important to be willing to step directly into one's pain and feel it in the way you need to.

Second it is imperative that one remains open for the healing to take place.

Third it is not necessary to have the whole process figured out at the very beginning.

Follow the process step by step and do what your soul is leading you to do. The process will unfold to lead you back to dry land. Although you may feel afraid, just follow your process.

Chapter 7

SOME FINAL HOPE-FILLED THOUGHTS

Looking back over our process so far, it becomes increasingly clear that healing had happened to us... It has only been the result of our willingness to open to it.

Staying Open to Healing
Grieving is not a linear process. Sometimes it feels as if it is all over the place. Some days one feels so good it is hard to believe you have been in so much pain only to be washed over by yet another wave.

One moment the sun shines and the next you find yourselves being hurled headlong back into the angry sea.

Wave by Wave - Forward & Backward
 - Upside Down
Yet bit by bit we find ourselves being healed. Our steps get lighter and some of the deep dark clouds lift.

Almost three years later, we now are not in as much pain. It seems that our pain has changed, transformed somehow into something much more gentle. We do not feel the wrenching that was once in our soul every time we saw a newborn child.

The pain we still feel is different now, somehow. So our emotions have moved from tremendous sadness every minute to experiencing that sadness only at certain times when we are reminded in a poignant way.

Pain Transforms
Often I look at Jayde's picture and a sigh passes my heart. Then I am also struck by the beauty of our two living children. At the same moment I am struck with the immensity of the blessing they now are to us. Then I realize that both are true, all at the same time.

Always Longing - Also Blessed
I see our little Keysha dressed up in her little dresses and our little Brenny playing in the sandbox, and I long to see Jayde here too. Sometimes I imagine how much fun they would have playing and dancing together.

I am also profoundly aware that in the midst of such a powerful call to keep on dancing from our little Jayde, that we have been prepared. Prepared for a little black-skinned, Haitian daughter who has an incredible dancing rhythm and a love for movement.

I watch our two children playing and giggling and I am reminded of the missing child. It brings such a mix of joy and sorrow... even now... just more gently.

Joy and Sorrow - Life Gifts Us
I miss buying her Christmas gifts, little cute clothes and birthday gifts. I miss watching her get them. I miss seeing her run and play in the snow and in the fall leaves. I miss seeing her dance with her daddy and brother and sister. I miss that we will never have a wedding nor will she stand up beside her sister at her wedding.

I miss her sitting up to the table and telling us of her day; telling of her first day of school; all of her firsts, her lasts and her everything.

I miss tucking her in at night. I miss her hugs and her I love you's. This is the void, yet it isn't an overwhelming void any more. Just the void of knowing just how important she is to us. The void of our precious one... no longer physically with us. A void that helps me stay open to the things in life that are important.

So she gifts us over and over and over in the void of her. It is all so very real. She remains so very real.

Embracing the Void
We live well now... within that void. We have stumbled our way back to the land of the living. It is within this void that we enter fully into life with one another and with our children. Laughing and delighting in our children, we go camping and enjoy the beauty of nature. In our leaving, we are reminded that we wish Jayde were coming too.

We tuck our kids in and we breathe thankful prayers for the blessings that are ours. And we are now able to listen to the grief of others like never before and that too is good. We experience the fear of losing in this way again. This too is living.

Just like the terror I felt the other day when our Brenny went missing close to the lake or when he ran away with his wagon in the midst of a busy crowd. So we hold still all the emotions of living: happiness, sadness, joy, fear, anger, etc.

Embracing Life's Imperfections
Joy and Sorrow... Opening and Closing... Life is made up of both. I think it is important for us all to begin to live in the reality that both are always true in life. If we can live in the imperfection of life and embrace it... we have truly learned to live. For these learned truths I am eternally grateful.

Entering into the Dance

"To die or to dance?"... A profound question for any one of us in life. Yet especially profound for those of us who are faced with intense loss. May you find some hope in these words. When you are ready, may you find your way clear to step boldly into your pain. In doing so, may you embrace the dance of life.

Finding Dry Land...

Chapter 7

-In Closing-
Tributes

IN CLOSING - TRIBUTES

To The Many Who Travelled With Us
We would never have made it through this journey, if it hadn't been for the many friends and family who journeyed with us. You cried with us, you held us, you fed us and cared for our son.

You stayed with us and listened and loved. You were the hand and heart of God for us and you helped to heal us. Thank you from the bottom of my heart for being so open.

Thanks to the **pastors, therapists** and other **professionals**; who stood by us to help us sort this whole grief thing out. Thank you for your wisdom and presence.

To My Partner and Soul-Mate
I am ever thankful to you my dear husband for loving me and for choosing to dance with me through this most difficult time. I would never have wanted to do this with anyone else but you. We have grown together through this process and I am blessed to share this life with you. Thank you for your undying love.

To Our Precious Children, Brendyn and Keysha
Thanks to my children. Brendyn for calling me to continue to live when every bone in my body

wanted to follow Jayde to heaven. Instead I knew you wanted my love and called it out. Your hugs comforted me and your life, called me to live. Thank you for your life that called me back to life.

I am thankful to my **Keysha**, our little adopted babe. You brought us so much life in the midst of such a painful time. Your coming reminded us to dance. You gave us a chance to cuddle a very little one when this experience had taken that from us so abruptly. I still love to hold you. You came just in time to remind us to stay open to loving. Thank you for gracing me with your presence.

To the Healer of Our Souls
For taking such good care of our baby girl, I am **deeply thankful to God**. Also for not leaving us, when we were in so much pain. For sending angels, friends, family and each other to hold us. I would never want to do a journey like this without you.

You held us, loved us, brought us hope and brought us healing. Thank you for giving us life and sending us who and what we needed. Most of all, thanks for not leaving us to drown at the bottom of our ocean.

You gifted us with our little Jayde. When she could not stay here with us; you allowed her to teach us, open us and remind us what life is all about. You used her life and leaving, to remind us of your great love. We are continually reminded to enter more fully into the dance of life, even in our void.

To Our Precious Jayde Mikayla

Jayde Mikayla... precious gem... we waited for you with such joyful anticipation. We had no idea just what an incredible gift you would be for us. Your gift came in disguise and at first we couldn't see the gift for the pain.

Your presence and your painful leaving taught us to live life more fully in the moment. From you we learned to trust deeply, to feel openly, to love when love is risky and to dance, even when our feet were dragging. You lived so closely to your maker and you brought us into that closeness even more deeply.

We will always miss you, our precious Jayde. Impatiently, we wait for the day when we will be reunited. We are deeply grateful for your time with us, although it was so very brief.

In Closing

We have grown to be grateful for the void you left us in. This void makes us eternally open to the "Lover of our Souls".

It allows us to journey more fully with others in their pain.

Best of all, we had the chance to love you and be loved by you.

Jayde... We will always miss you at our table, on our holidays, on our celebrations, and every day. My soul longs for you... to hold you. Yet I will always, always hold you in my heart.

Thank you my baby, my wise, wise little baby girl. May you find dancing shoes in heaven until we are able to dance with you there.

-In Closing-
For Your Journey

IN CLOSING – FOR YOUR JOURNEY

I often think of those who are freshly grieving.

When I hear that one of you has lost someone, my heart aches for you - with you. I know you have such a difficult journey to live through. I know your deep, deep ocean is feeling bottomless.

Also I know that you can do this. Healing is coming your way. One day if you allow it, you will find your own dance of wholeness. For now you just need to be in the midst of the ocean, until it is time.

The most difficult decision any of us can make in these times...
is to choose life.

Choose to dance when our feet just don't want to do so.

May you find the strength to be fully in your grieving and fully in your living.

So keep on breathing and let it unfold.

You are not alone.

In Closing

Some "Rememberings" For Your Ocean Journey

You are not alone.
Reach out to those who care for you.
Stay open to the love...

Breathe...

Let it unfold...

Choose to Dance...

Allow yourself to step into your pain...

There are no rules...Do what you need to do...
Trust your process...

You will heal...that is how you are created...
How well you heal is your choice.

Be in your pain...Don't try to avoid it or fix it.

Don't be afraid to open to the gifts life might have to offer you...

Just BE...

For Your Journey

I wish you peace as you journey through this deep, deep dark ocean of your grief. I know you will find your way back to dry land.

-In Closing-

Final Poem

Finding self back on Dry Land.

Solid ground beneath me
looking o'er the sea from shore
at this journey oh so long....

sun shining now through rain
joy has reached my wrenching soul

Remembering

... now with lesser pain...

but still a void
that ne're shall go...
yet always with me is that love…

As I release my hurt
... comes joy

as I embrace my pain
... comes life

and my heart
smiles...

and my feet
dance...

ISBN 1412069661